stars and Constellations

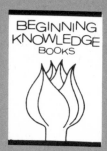

Beginning Knowledge Books are for the young reader who is eager to learn about the world around him. Beautiful color illustrations and simple words are guides that offer a wealth of carefully chosen answers for young questioners. The editors of the Beginning Knowledge Books are grateful for the expert assistance of: Miss Amy Clampitt, formerly Librarian, National Audubon Society, in checking the text; Paul B. G. Twomey, formerly Planetarium Director, Corpus Christi Public Schools.

The Beginning Knowledge Book of
Stars and Constellations

by Ann Ivins/Illustrated by Robert Galandak and José Vides

CONTENTS

POLARIS IN URSA MINOR

SIRIUS IN CANIS MAJOR

PROCYON IN CANIS MINOR

RIGEL IN ORION

CAPELLA IN AURIGA

ALDEBARAN IN TAURUS

CASTOR AND POLLUX IN GEMINI

REGULUS IN LEO

SPICA IN VIRGO

ARCTURUS IN BOOTES

VEGA IN LYRA

DENEB IN CYGNUS

ALTAIR IN AQUILA

ANTARES IN SCORPIO

FOMALHAUT IN PISCIS AUSTRINUS

ALPHA CRUCIS IN CRUX

ACHERNAR IN ERIDANUS

CANOPUS IN CARINA

A RUTLEDGE BOOK

Copyright 1969 in all countries of the International
Copyright Union by Rutledge Books, Inc.
Prepared and produced for Crowell-Collier Press, New York
Collier-Macmillan Ltd., London
The Macmillan Company
Collier-Macmillan Canada Ltd., Toronto, Ontario
Library of Congress Catalog Card Number: 68-10732

Printed and bound by Arnoldo Mondadori, Verona, Italy
First Printing

Stars and Constellations

Everything in space is far away from everything else. And everything in space is always moving. Even the stars move. They seem to stand still only because of the enormous distances between them. Astronomers— scientists who study the stars through telescopes— tell us that some of the stars are moving toward us, others away from us, at tremendous speeds.

And, of course, the earth is moving, too. Along with the rest of the planets, it spins like a top and at the same time travels around the sun. Because of the earth's movements, many of the stars we see at the same hour of the night are different throughout the year. So we speak of winter stars, spring stars, summer stars and autumn stars.

But from the United States there are stars that can be seen all night, all year around. These are the circumpolar stars.

Long ago, men looking at the night sky saw groups of stars that seemed to belong together. In these groups they imagined they saw the outlines of birds, animals, humans, or objects. These groups, called constellations, are named after these figures.

When we look at the stars in the night sky, the one we know best cannot be seen—our sun.

Of all the stars that can be seen at night the one nearest to the earth is Alpha Centauri, in the constellation Centaurus, about 26,000,000,000,000

miles away. Its companion, Proxima Centauri, revolves

around it, just as the moon goes around

the earth. Proxima Centauri is nearer, but so much

smaller that it can be seen only through a telescope.

Some stars are about the diameter—the

measurement, edge to edge, through the center—

of the earth, which measures about 8,000 miles.

These are known as dwarf stars. Others, the giants

and supergiants, are millions of miles in diameter.

Our sun, with a diameter of 864,000 miles, is neither

a giant nor a dwarf, but somewhere in between.

Size and distance are not the only reasons

some stars appear brighter than others. They may

also be brighter because they are so very hot.

All the stars we see are globes of flaming gas

just as the sun is. But they are not all the same temperature. The very hottest may have a surface temperature of 80,000 degrees Fahrenheit. The light from these stars is bluish-white or blue. Medium-hot stars shine with a yellow light—the sun is one of these. Still others are reddish. They are known as "cool" stars—although they may have temperatures of 3,000 degrees or more.

Seen from the earth, each star appears as a tiny pinpoint of light. But many of the stars are really double—actually a pair of stars that are moving around each other. There are even multiple stars—three or four or more all traveling around one another, yet millions of miles apart.

This book shows only a few of the many, many stars and constellations.

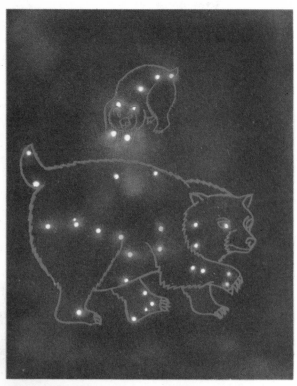

Because the earth "wobbles," the Pole Star is not always the same star. In 10,000 years Deneb will be near the Pole. Perhaps it will be called the Pole Star.

Polaris, the north or polestar, appears to stay in almost the same spot all night and at all seasons of the year, because its place in relation to the earth is almost directly above the North Pole. It is part of the constellation Ursa Minor — Latin for smaller bear — also known as the Little Dipper.

The circumpolar stars of the Big Dipper, in the constellation Ursa Major, appear to move in a circle around Polaris. To find the polestar in the night sky, first look for the Big Dipper. The two end stars in the bowl of the Dipper seem to form a line pointing to the star at the tip of the handle of the Little Dipper. That is Polaris.

Polaris is a large star. It is also a double star—two globes of flaming gas.

Sirius
in Canis Major

Sirius is 26 times brighter than
the sun. It looks fainter because
it is farther away from the earth.

In the northern hemisphere, the
brightest star is Sirius, a blue-white
star a little larger than the sun
and twice as hot.

Sirius is called the dog star — it
is part of the constellation Canis
Major—bigger dog.

The best time to see it is from
January to March, around 10 in the
evening in the southeast.

Sirius is the bright star of a
double star system. Its companion
is a white dwarf, "The Pup."

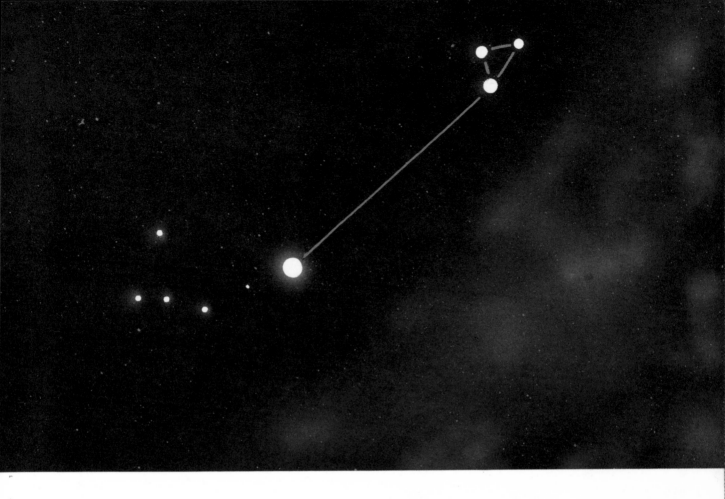

Procyon in Canis Minor

The surface temperature of Procyon is about 7,500 degrees C. The sun's temperature is about 6,000 degrees.

In the constellation Canis Minor —smaller dog—the brightest star is Procyon. Its name, a Greek word meaning "leading dog," was given it because it appears above the horizon about 40 minutes before Sirius. The best time to look for it is from December to May.

Among all the stars in the sky, Procyon is 8th brightest. It is a yellowish-white star twice the size of the sun. It, too, is the bright star of a double star system.

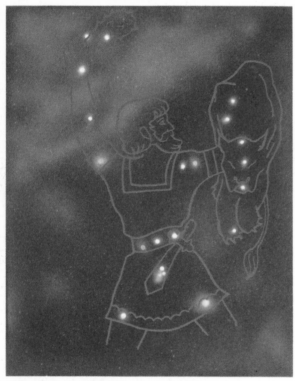

Rigel is as bright as 50,000 suns put together. Betelgeuse, a "variable" star that swells and shrinks, is on the tunic cuff on Orion's left arm.

The constellation Orion can best be seen in the winter sky. It takes its name from a mighty hunter. According to one Greek legend, Diana killed him by accident and placed him in the sky.

In old star maps Orion was shown as a man carrying a club, with a sword hanging from his belt. Three stars in a row form the belt.

Below the belt is Rigel, the 7th brightest star. It is a large blue-white star, 33 times the diameter of the sun.

Above the belt is Betelgeuse, the name Arabian astronomers gave to the 9th brightest star. It is a red supergiant, around 400 times the size of the sun. Even though it is so much bigger than Rigel, Betelgeuse is less bright because it is cooler.

Capella
in Auriga

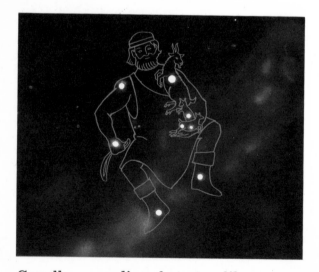

Capella, a medium-hot star like
the sun, is as bright as 200 suns
put together because it is bigger.

The constellation Auriga — the
charioteer — can best be seen from
October through April. It contains
the 6th brightest star, Capella, a
large yellow star.

In the same constellation is a
double star, Epsilon Aurigae. The
larger of the two globes that make
up Epsilon Aurigae is about 3,000
times the diameter of the sun—but
it cannot be seen, even with a
telescope, because its temperature
is so low and its gases so thin.

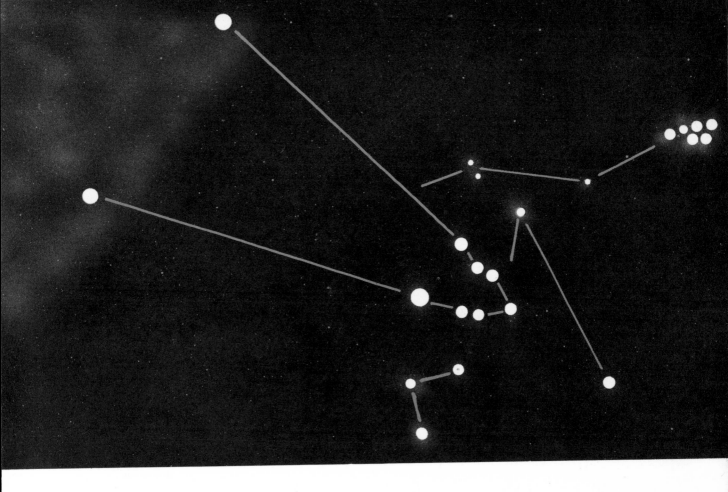

Aldebaran in Taurus

Star cluster Pleiades, near Aldebaran, forms the bull's shoulder. Star cluster Hyades forms the bull's face.

The 14th brightest star in the night sky is Aldebaran, Arabic for "follower." Taurus means "bull." It rises an hour after the star cluster Pleiades, from 250 to 300 stars that travel together through space. However, not all the stars in the cluster called Pleiades can be seen with the naked eye.

Aldebaran, an orange-red giant, is the brightest star in the bull's face. It can best be seen from October through March.

The twins are in the path of the planets. Two of our planets, Uranus in 1781 and Pluto in 1930, were discovered when they were passing through Gemini.

The two brightest stars in the constellation Gemini, the twins, are Castor and Pollux. On old star maps one twin was shown as a boxer and the other as a horseman.

The brighter of the two is yellow-orange Pollux. It is 17th brightest among the stars. Castor ranks 22nd, and is a multiple star — actually six flaming globes, consisting of three pairs. In each pair, the two stars revolve about each other and the three pairs all revolve around one another as well.

In Roman mythology, Castor and Pollux were twin sons of Jupiter, the ruler of the gods.

The rest of the stars in Gemini are much fainter and can be seen only on a clear, moonless night. The best time to look for the twins is from December to May.

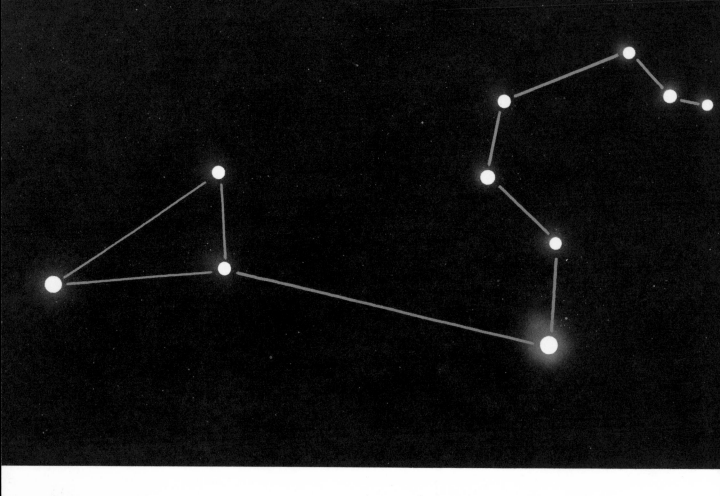

Regulus
in Leo

Leo looks more like a question mark
turned around than a lion. Regulus
is the end of the tail.

One of the bright stars in the
spring sky is a blue-white triple
star, Regulus. Its gases are so
thin that its smaller but brighter
companion can sometimes be seen
through it. Regulus belongs to the
constellation Leo, the lion, which
is most easily seen on nights from
February through June.

Regulus is a Latin word
meaning "prince" or "little king."
The star was named by Copernicus,
the "father of modern astronomy."

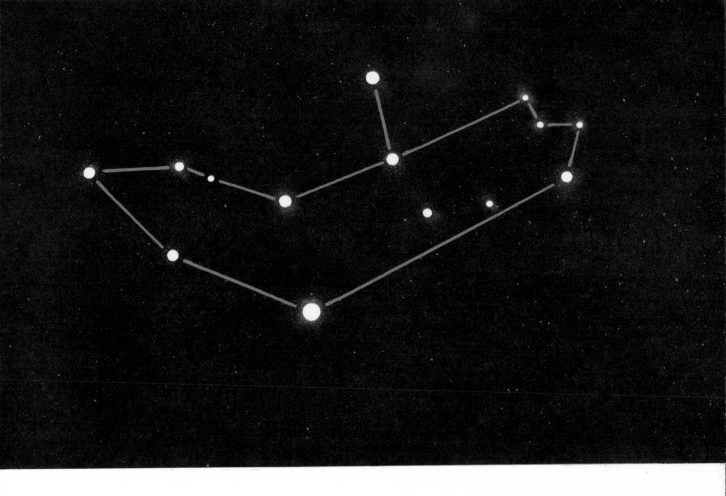

Spica
in Virgo

Spica, with a surface temperature of 15,000-30,000 degrees, is 1,000 times as bright as the sun.

The brilliant blue-white star Spica appears in the sky before midnight in April, May and June. It belongs to the constellation Virgo, the virgin. She is shown in old star maps as a woman holding a sheaf of wheat.

Spica, 15th in brightness, is a double star of medium size. As the two stars circle each other, the brighter one is sometimes hidden by the dimmer one, and Spica is less bright for a time.

One of the oldest identified constellations, Boötes looks more like a kite than a herdsman. Arcturus is the bright star at the hem of the herdsman's tunic.

Arcturus, a reddish-orange giant, is 35 times the diameter of the sun. Although it is cooler than the sun, it is 100 times as bright because of its size. It is a part of the constellation Boötes, the herdsman.

In July and August, Arcturus is one of the first stars to appear, high in the sky, soon after sunset. It is 4th brightest of all the stars. To find it, look for the Big Dipper and follow the curve of the handle away from the Dipper's bowl. The star that appears just beyond is Arcturus. It appears to follow the bear of Ursa Major—and the name Arcturus, from the Greek, means "bear keeper."

Speeding along at 85 miles per second, Arcturus is one of the fastest-moving stars in the night sky and one of our nearest neighbors.

Vega
in Lyra

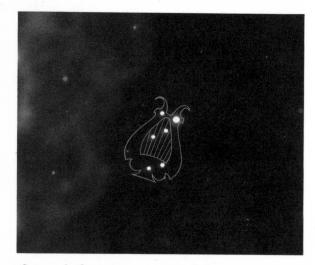

One of the stars nearest to earth, in 1850 Vega was the first star to be photographed.

Vega, a brilliant blue-white star, is 5th in brightness. It is hotter than the sun and 50 times as bright. It is in the constellation Lyra, the lyre. Lyra is the Greek word for lyre, a musical instrument similar to the harp.

Vega, which is an Arabic word that means "falling eagle," can be seen straight overhead from May through November. With the help of .field glasses its bluish color will be more easily visible.

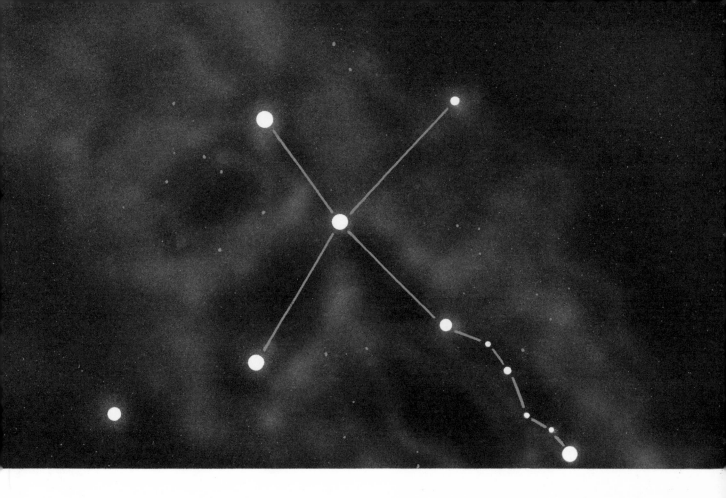

Deneb
in Cygnus

Cygnus, the swan, is also called
the Northern Cross. Deneb, brighter
than 10,000 suns, is at its top.

The constellation Cygnus, the swan, does look rather like the graceful bird for which it was named. The brightest star in Cygnus is Deneb, shown in old maps of the sky as a part of the tail—and "tail" is what Deneb means in Arabic.

A blue-white star, Deneb is so tremendously hot that it ranks 19th in brightness, even though it is 9,600,000,000,000,000 miles away. It can best be seen in the night sky from June through November.

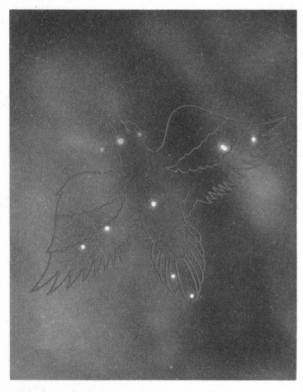

One constellation that seems to have a name that "fits" is Aquila, the eagle. With Altair to lead the way, the "eagle" really does seem to soar high in the sky.

The constellation Aquila, the eagle, is part of the beauty of the night sky from July through early October.

Part of the head of the eagle is Altair, the brightest star in this constellation. Two fainter stars appear on either side of it. Altair is the Arabic for "the flier."

Altair is a large white star and is 12th in brightness. It is 9 times as bright as the sun. It is one of the stars nearest to earth and is traveling nearer every year at a speed of 1,000 miles a minute.

Along with Deneb in the constellation Cygnus and with Vega in Lyra, Altair forms what is known as the summer triangle—three bright stars that sailors look for to help them in finding their way.

Antares
in Scorpio

Low in the sky near the horizon,
Antares, "heart" of the scorpion,
glows red in the southern sky.

The supergiant Antares is 480 times the diameter of the sun. A double star, its red glare often hides its tiny green companion.

Antares is in the constellation Scorpio, the scorpion, and can be seen in southern skies during July and August. Antares ranks 16th in brightness. When it is in the same part of the sky as the planet Mars, also red, the star is sometimes mistaken for the planet. Its name, Antares, means "rival of Mars."

Fomalhaut in Piscis Austrinus

As bright as 13 suns,
Formalhaut is another star that
is near the planet earth.

In the southern skies of autumn, from September through November, the red star Fomalhaut can be seen near the horizon soon after dark.

It is the brightest star of the constellation Piscis Austrinus, the southern fish. Fomalhaut is an Arabic word.

Although Fomalhaut ranks 18th in brightness, it is less easy to see in the northern hemisphere than many other stars because it is so low in the sky.

Beta Crucis is at the tip of the left arm of the cross. Alpha Crucis is just above the Centaur's right front hoof. Alpha and Beta Centauri are in the left hind leg.

In the southern hemisphere, the best-known constellation is Crux, the southern cross. It contains the 13th brightest star, Acrux or Alpha Crucis, a bluish triple star. At the tip of the eastern arm of the cross is Beta Crucis, the 20th star in brightness.

Almost surrounding the southern cross is an enormous constellation, Centaurus, the centaur, named for a creature in Greek mythology that was half man, half horse. In what old star maps show as its hind leg are Alpha Centauri, 3rd brightest of the stars, and Beta Centauri, 11th in brightness.

These stars can be seen all year in the southern hemisphere. In the northern hemisphere Alpha Centauri can be seen in the month of May.

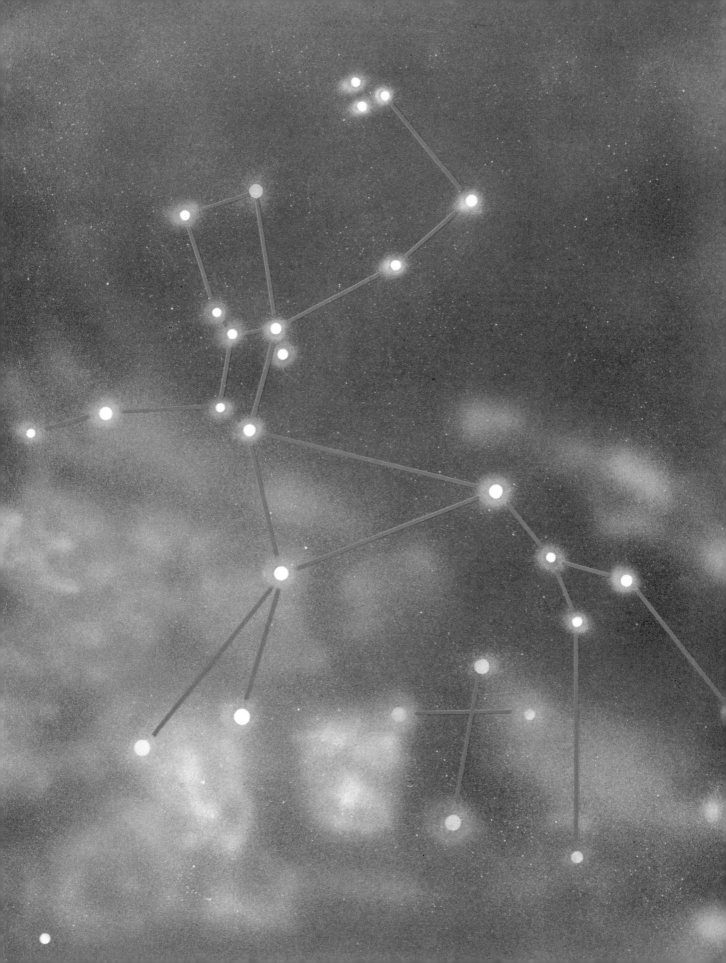

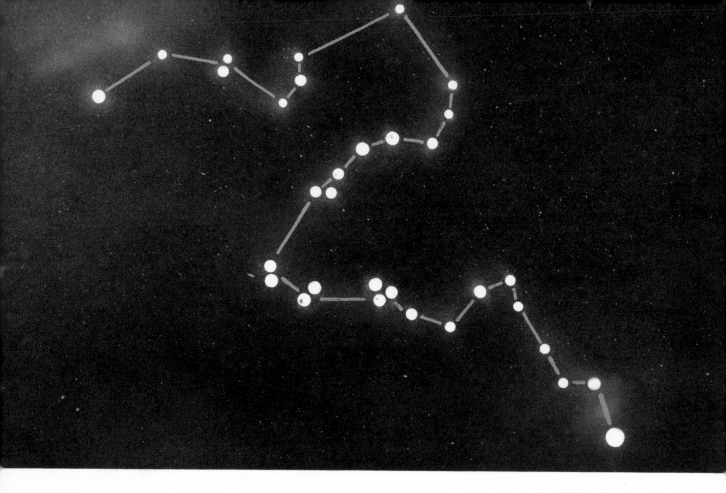

Achernar in Eridanus

Achernar, 200 times as bright
as the sun, has a surface
temperature of 15,500 degrees.

Curving across the sky, the constellation Eridanus suggests the course of a river. It begins near the star Rigel in Orion, and ends with the star Achernar—an Arabic word that means "end of the river."

Although Achernar, a large bluish star, is the 10th brightest, it is too far to the south to be seen easily in most parts of the northern hemisphere. But in the southern United States it can sometimes be seen in the fall.

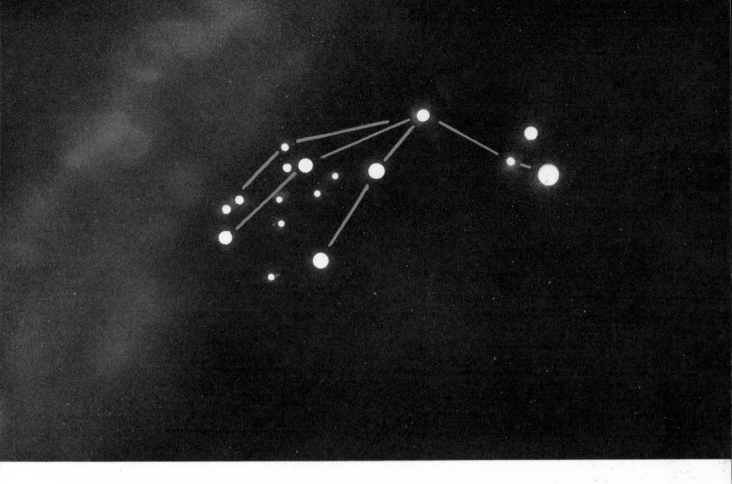

Canopus in Carina

In the southern skies, Canopus, the second brightest star, is 2,000 times as bright as the sun.

The constellation Carina, the ship's keel, is a familiar sight in the southern hemisphere's sky. It belongs to a larger group of stars, Argo Navis, or the ship Argo.

In the keel is the star Canopus, a yellow-white supergiant second only to Sirius in brightness, and 210 times the diameter of the sun.

Canopus cannot easily be seen in most of the northern hemisphere. The best time to look for it is during December and January.